100 Easy Blues Harmonica Licks for Diaton
By
Yvonnick Prene

nyharmonicaschool.com
yprene@gmail.com

Copyright © 2015 by Yvonnick Prene
Cover Illustration, book design and production
Photo by Tony Tixier. Editing by Gisela Adisa.

Table of Content

About The Author 3

Introduction 4

How To Use This Book 5

Audio Examples 6

Basic Harmonica Techniques 6

Howlin' Wolf
Patterns in the style of Howlin'Wolf 12

Slim Harpo
Patterns in the style of Slim Harpo 14

Junior Wells
Patterns in the style of Junior Wells 17

J-J Milteau
Patterns in the style of Jean-Jacques Milteau 21

Sonny Boy Williamson
Patterns in the style of Sonny Boy Williamson 23

Little Walter
Patterns in the style of Little Walter 25

Big Walter Horton
Patterns in the style of Big Walter 27

James Cotton
Patterns in the style of James Cotton 30

Fundamentals Harmonica Scales

The Major Scale 33

The Major Pentatonic Scale 35

The Blues Scale 36

The Melodic Minor Scale 36

The Dorian Mode 37

The Mixolydian Mode 38

The Bebop Dominant Scale 39

The D Minor Pentatonic Scale 39

The G Major Pentatonic 40

Audio Examples

Audio Examples **41**

Biography

Since moving to New York City, composer and educator Yvonnick Prene has become one of the rising stars in the harmonica world and a sideman in demand. He has recorded three albums as a leader and been working with todays top jazz artists such as Kevin Hays, Rich Perry, Mike Moreno, Peter Bernstein, Aaron Parks, Jon Cowherd, Laurent Cugny, Steve Cardenas, Vic Juris, Alex Tassel and Scott Tixier among others. Yvonnick was born in Paris, France on January 19. He began as a guitarist, later switching to the diatonic harmonica, and eventually settling on the chromatic harmonica as his primary instrument. He first began playing the harmonica professionally in Parisian clubs at 17, then started his studies at Sorbonne University, from which he received a master's degree in music (2011). While still enrolled at the Sorbonne, Prené relocated to New York City and was awarded multiple full-tuition scholarships at The City College of New York, (MICEFA, 2007), Columbia University (Alliance Program, 2008) and at the New School for Jazz and Contemporary Music (Merit-Based Scholarship, 2009) where he had the opportunity to study with Lee Konitz and Reggie Workman among others. In 2012 he earned a bachelor's degree in music from The New School for Jazz & Contemporary Music. Yvonnick is the founder of New York Harmonica School, the first harmonica school in NYC. Yvonnick is currently based in Manhattan, New York.

Discography

Yvonnick Prene, Breathe, 2016
Yvonnick Prene, Merci Toots, 2015
Yvonnick Prene & Padam Swing, "Wonderful World", 2014
Yvonnick Prene, "Jour de Fete", SteepleChase Records, 2013

Bibliography

100 Jazz Patterns for Chromatic Harmonica, Vol 1, Amazon
100 Jazz Patterns for Chromatic Harmonica, Vol 2, Amazon
Classical Themes for Chromatic Harmonica, Amazon
Jazz Etudes for Chromatic Harmonica, Amazon

Introduction

"...The harmonica is the mother of the band, once you got a good harp, you're in business..."
Otis Spann (Muddy Water's pianist)

This book is designed to for the beginning and intermediate level harmonica players, it contains an encyclopedia of blues phrases they can learn and use while improvising alone or with a band. The great harmonica player often mixed spontaneous original ideas with well known licks to create new solos. Most of the time licks and riffs are "borrowed", adapted, and changed into new ones. It is rare when someone comes up with a totally fresh approach without relying on the tradition meaning blues phrases, riffs, and also scales. The following licks were inspired by musical improvisations of blues legends such as Junior Wells, Sonny Boy Williamson II, Little Walter, Jean-Jacques Milteau, Big Walter Horton, James Cotton, Howlin' Wolf and Paul Butterfield.

At the end of the book, you will find a Dropbox link to download over 100 audio examples. I hope this book will provide inspiration and a practical method for blues improvising on the diatonic harmonica. Easy Blues Harmonica Licks will work with any 10 hole chromatic harmonica in the key of C.

LISTEN-IMITATE-RECREATE

How To Use This Book

"Blues is easy to play, but hard to feel". Jimi Hendrix

1) Listen to the audio example before playing the pattern
All of the material presented should be sung and played along with the audio examples with your harmonica. It is a sure way to refine your capacity to hear intervals and recognize pitch. It will also without any doubt improve your time feel and technic. Play along with my performance of the patterns and scales until you get it to sit right in the rhythmic pocket. Try to match my rhythmic "feel" and articulation perfectly and move from note to note with a legato phrasing. If you have to skip one or more holes always keep your mouth on the harmonica and slide it smoothly to the note desired.

2) Practice with a metronome
Play it rubato at first, meaning without a pulsation in order to focus only on sight-reading the notes. Then you should practice with the metronome at a slow tempo then gradually augment speed. Time and rhythm are number one. All note seem to sound good when they are interpreted with "good time". Practicing slowly is the key to certain progress.

You can set the metronome at 45bpm, the metronome clicking on beats 2 and 4. It will develop your "time-feel" and make you a stronger player when you'll be improvising with a band.

3) Repetition & Memorization
Once the pattern is memorized in the written key try to transpose it to a different key by switching to a different harmonica. For example a harmonica in the key of G or A.

4) Don't forget the Greats!
Listen to the founding fathers of Blues Harmonica such as Little Walter, Sonny Boy Williamson, Junior Wells, Jimmy Reed, Big Walter…and make music! Play with other musicians if you can. Otherwise I recommend practicing improvisation by playing over blues tracks.

5) A few tips…
Avoid playing while bending down your head otherwise the saliva will fall into the harmonica.
When you play several blow or inhale notes in a row, don't interrupt your breathing but move slightly the harmonica.

To see the musical example in a larger format (Kindle Version), click on it. Good luck and have fun!

Audio Examples in Mp3 Format Available to Download Here

Enter this link into your browser:

https://nyharmonicaschool.com/audio/

Or

https://goo.gl/MMrP3h

Nomenclature:

() The numbers between the parentheses indicate a draw note.
Bends: The **+** sign in front a number represents a note being bended down a half step
= Indicates to bend a step down, **#** represents a note being bended down a step and half

Holding the harmonica:

1) Form a C shape with your index finger and thumb, then lay the harmonica on top of it. Hold it between the index finger and thumb. In this picture, you can see a 10 hole diatonic harmonica. The other hand comes behind the harmonica to form a cup in order to better control the sound. Then bring the harp to your lips, always wet, to facilitate sliding up and down and assure the best airtightness.

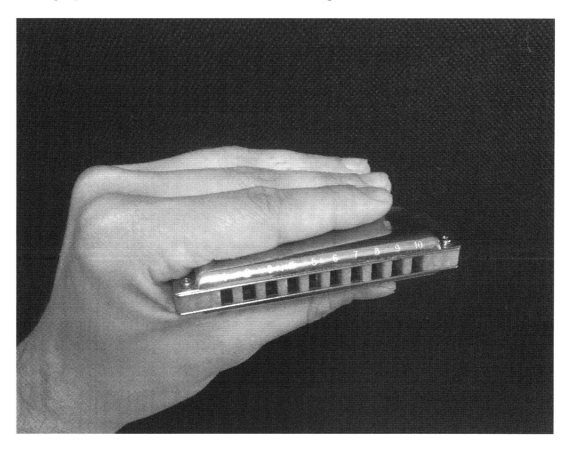

C Diatonic Harmonica Lay Out

Notes of a C-10 holes diatonic harmonica:

Hole	1	2	3	4	5	6	7	8	9	10
Draw	D	G	B	D	F	A	B	D	F	A
Blow	C	E	G	C	E	G	C	E	G	C

Track 1:

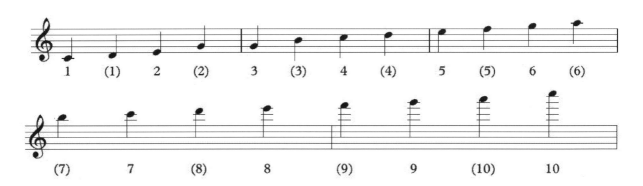

Notes of a C-10 holes diatonic harmonica with "bendings":

Hole	1	2	3	4	5	6	7	8	9	10
Bend 3rd level			Ab							
Bends 2nd Level		F	A							
Bends 1st Level	Db	Gb	Bb	Db		Ab				
Draw	D	G	B	D	F	A	B	D	F	A
Blow	C	E	G	C	E	G	C	E	G	C

Track 2:

Keys of Harmonica and Positions:

Blues harmonica players talk about "position" to designate the tonality in which they're playing in. For example in a harmonica in C Major 1st position is C, 2nd position is G Major and the third position in D minor.

Harmonica in…	Playing in 1st Position in the key of…	Playing in 2nd Position (cross harp) in the key of…	Playing in 3rd Position in the key of…
C	C major	G major	D
Db	Db major	Ab major	Eb
Eb	D major	A major	E
E	Eb major	Bb major	F
F	E major	B major	F#
Gb	F major	C major	G
G	Gb major	D major	Ab
Tonic (The first note of the scale)	1st and 4th Hole Blow	2nd Hole Draw	1st and 4th Hole Draw
Example of songs	Michael Row The Boat Ashore	Juke	The Thrill Is Gone
Particularities	Using mostly blow notes	Using mostly draw notes	Played more often from draw hole 4 to 7
Styles	Folk & Pop	Blues & Jazz	Minor Songs

Single Notes:

To play a clean single note, push out your lips and pronounce "woo" as seen on the photo in order to get a small hole to blow or inhale through. If you are having difficulty playing the 1 or 2 or 3-draw hole, it's normal. Most beginners find it very difficult to get a clear note on these holes. So try breathing softer with less air, from the bottom of your mouth, instead of, sucking the air from the lips, which is only recommended when you want to bend, the pitch goes lower if you "suck in" the note.

WAH WAH Effect

Track 3

This remarkably effect is commonly used in blues. It is obtained by opening and closing the hands while you're playing the harmonica.

First, hold your harmonica in your left hand. Secondly, wrap your right hand around the harp as to form a cup shape in order to create a resonance chamber. Then draw simultaneously in holes (3), (4) and (5) while saying OO-WAH. Close your right hand when saying OO, and open it when saying WAH.

CLOSE:

OPEN:

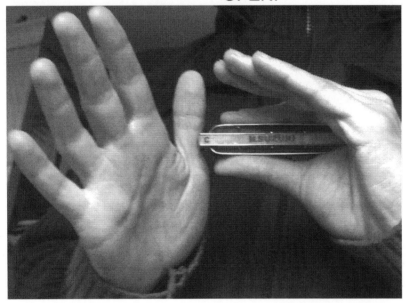

The Shake (Trill)
Track 4

You just draw in on the harmonica on hole 4 and move the harp to the 5 draw. Repeat this movement back and forth across your mouth with your hands. Start slowly at the beginning and make sure to play each not individually before going to the next.

Bending:

To obtain a bend notated + or - try to pronounce "e-u" or "te-u" in the harmonica on hole 1. Then try the on holes 4, 6, 3 and 2.

Make sure you're drawing in a single hole. Breath in while saying "i". "I" corresponds to the natural note, continue to inhale and pronounce "u" . "U" is the bent note. You should feel your tongue moving slowly to the back of your throat while lowering the pitch of a note. The lower the note, the movement of the tongue is deeper. Try also to breath in a bit stronger and hold a bit more the harmonica against your lips a bit more. Another method consist of whistling while breathing in and lowering the pitch of the note you're whistling.

To check if your bends are in tune, you can use a chromatic tuner, a piano app or another instrument while bending on your harmonica. If the two sounds match perfectly you're doing good! Otherwise you can move your tongue position up or down your tongue position a little to achieve the notes you want.

Track 5
Bending Hole 1 from D to Db

Track 6
Bending Hole 2 from G to F# and F# to F

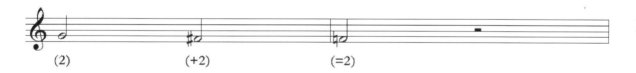

Track 7
Bending Hole 3 from B to Bb, Bb to A and A to Ab

Track 8
Bending Hole 4 from D to C#

Track 9
Bending Hole 6 from A to Ab

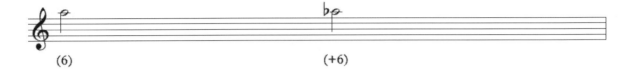

(6)   (+6)

Patterns in the style of Howlin' Wolf

"See, the blues is a thing that will make you sing. You sing the way you feel."
Howlin' Wolf

Perhaps better known for his unique singing and pioneer work on the electric guitar, Howling Wolf was nonetheless a formidable harmonica player. He learned his craft in the 30s from Delta blues master, Sonny Boy Williamson (Aleck "Rice" Miller) who married his half-sister. His hits include "How Many More Years," "Smokestack Lightnin","Sitting on Top of the World." "Spoonful," among others titles on Chess Records.

Track 10:

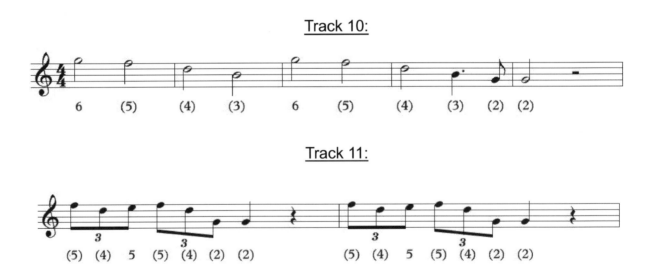

6   (5)   (4)   (3)   6   (5)   (4)   (3)   (2) (2)

Track 11:

(5) (4) 5 (5) (4) (2) (2)   (5) (4) 5 (5) (4) (2) (2)

Track 12:

Track 13:

Track 14:

Track 15:

Track 16:

Track 17:

6 6 6 6 6 (5) (4) (5) (4)   2 3 (3) 4 4 4 4 4 (4) (3) (2) (2)

Track 18:

3 3 (3) (3) 4 4 (4)   (4)   4 (3) 3 3 (3) (3) 4 4 (4)   (4)

Track 19:

6   6 (5) (4) 4 (3) 6   6 (5) (4) 4 (3)

Track 20:

8 9   (6) (7) (8) (7) 6 (6) 6 5   8 9   (6) (7) (8) (7) 6 (6) 6 5

Track 21:

(4) (5)   (4) (5)   6   6   (4) (5)   (4) (5)   6   6

Track 22:

(5) (4) (5) (4) (5) (4) (5) 6   6 6 (5) (4) (5) (4) (5) (4) (5) (4) (5) 6   6 6 (5) (4)

<u>Recommended Listening</u>: Howlin' Wolf: His Best -Chess 50th Anniversary
Collection, Chess, 1997

<u>Patterns in the style of Slim Harpo (1924-1970)</u>

**"Music was the only thing I had. When I got my harp I'd listen to songs real close
on the radio and learn them, then I'd play it on the harp." Slim Harpo**

Born in Los Angeles, Harpo played both guitar and neck-rack harmonica melting Rock roll rhythm, with Blues. As critic Peter Guralnick put it, it was "as if a black country and western singer or a white rhythm and blues singer were attempting to impersonate a member of the opposite genre". His bigger successes were "Rainin' In My Heart" and "I'm a King Bee" and gave him an international reputation. Especially in the UK where Harpo influenced many rockers such as Mike Jagger, the Kinks and The Yardbirds.

Track 23:

Track 24:

Track 25:

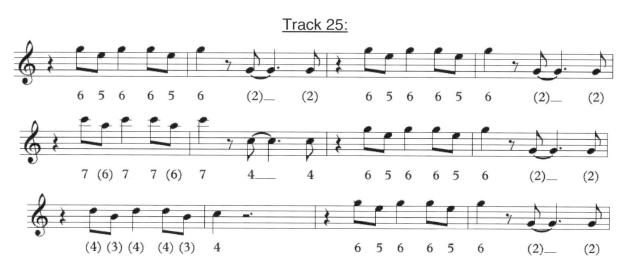

Track 26:

Track 27:

6   (5)__   (4) 4   (3)   3   3   6   (5)__ (4) 4   (3)   3   3

Track 28:

(5) (4) (5) (4) (5) (4) (5) (4) 4 (3) 3   (5) (4) (5) (4) (5) (4) (5) (4) 4 (3) 3

Track 29:

3   3   (4) 5 6   3   3   3   3   3   (4) 5 6   3   3   (4) 5 6

4   4   6 (6) 7   4   4   6 (6) 7   3   3   (4) 5 6   3   3   (4) 5 6

(4)   (4) (6) (7) (8) 4   4   6 (6) 7   3   3   (4) 5 6   3   3   (4) 5 6

Track 30:

(2) (3) (4) (5)   5 (4) (2)   (2)   (2) (3) (4) (5)   5

Track 31:

(2)   (3)   (2)   (2)   (+3)   (2)

Track 32:

3   (3) (4)   5   6   5   (4) (3)   3   (3) (4)   5   6   5   (4) (3)

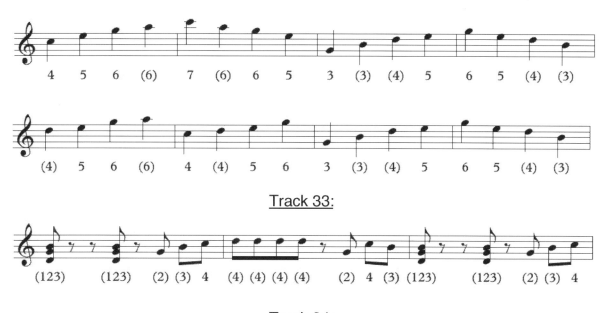

Track 33:

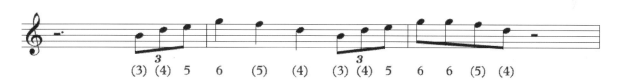

Track 34:

Track 35:

Track 36:

Recommended Listening: Slim Harpo, Best of Slim Harpo, Hip-O, 1996

Patterns in the style of Junior Wells (1934-1998)

"I go no place, night or day without having my harmonica in my pocket".
Junior Wells

At barely ten, Junior Wells was already playing harmonica in the streets of Memphis, like his hero Sonny Boy Williamson, whom he met when he moved to Chicago in 1946. With the likes of Big Walter Horton, Little Walter, and Howlin' Wolf Junior Wells is one of the most gifted harmonica and most active of the emergent electric Chicago blues scene.

<u>Track 37:</u>

Here is a simple blues using holes 1, 2, and 3 played simultaneously.

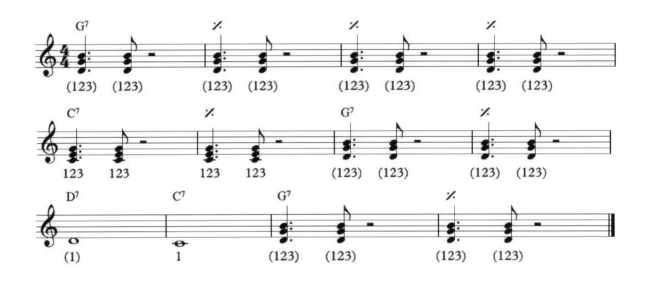

<u>Track 38:</u>

<u>Track 39:</u>

<u>Track 40:</u>

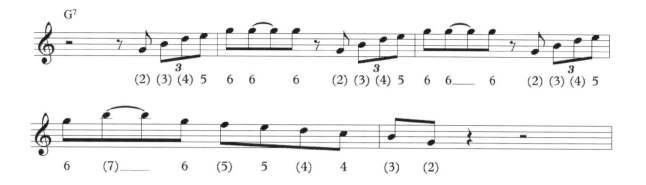

Track 41:

Track 42:

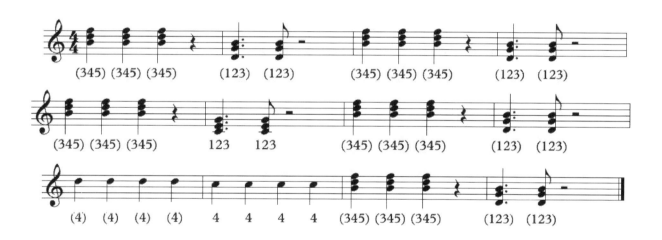

Track 43:

Track 44:

Track 45:

Track 46:

Track 47:

Track 48:

Recommended Listening: Junior Wells, It's My Life, Baby, Vanguard, 1988

Patterns in the style of Jean-Jacques Milteau (1950)

It will never be a saxophone , it will never be a violin, a piano ever. As against it is a sound, a sound specificity and above all a historical specificity. Jean-Jacques Milteau

Jean-Jacques Milteau is a French blues harmonica player, singer, and songwriter who has recorded dozens of albums and collaborated with high-profile French and American artists such as Yves Montand, Keb Mo, Charles Aznavour, Jean-Jacques Goldman. He has won prestigious award and is regarded as one of the best European blues harp players.

Track 49:

(1) 2 3 2 (1) 2 (3) 2 (5) 6 (5) 5 (5) 6 (5) 5 (4)

Track 50:

6 5 (5) 5 (4) 5 (4) 4 (4) 4 (3) 6 5 (5) 5 (4) 5 (4) 4 (4) 4 (3)

Track 51:

(4) (+4) (4) (+4) (3) 3 (4) (+4) (4) (+4) (3) 3

Track 52:

6 (5) 6 (5) (4) 6 6 (5) 6 (5) 5 (2) (=2) (2) (=2) (1) (2) (2) (+2) (2) (+2) (1)

Track 53:

6 (5) (4) 6 (5) (4) 5 (4)   6 (5) (4) 6 (5) (4) 5 (4)   (3) 3 3 3

Track 54:

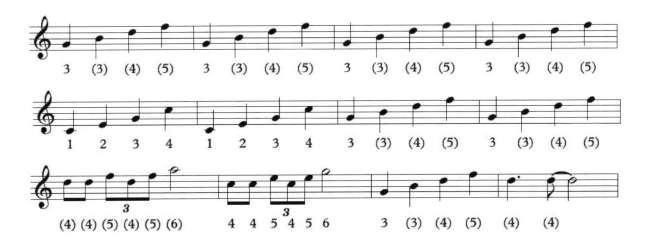

3 (3) (4) (5)   3 (3) (4) (5)   3 (3) (4) (5)   3 (3) (4) (5)

1 2 3 4   1 2 3 4   3 (3) (4) (5)   3 (3) (4) (5)

(4) (4) (5) (4) (5) (6)   4 4 5 4 5 6   3 (3) (4) (5) (4) (4)

Track 55:

(7) (8) (7) (8) (7) (6) 6   (7) (8) (7) (8) (7) (6) 6   (7) (7) 8 (8)

Track 56:

(123) x3___ (123) x3___ (123) (2) (3) 4 (45)   (123) x3   (123)x3

Track 57:

(1) 2 3 (3) (4) (3) 4 (4)   (3) 3 2 (1) 2 3 (3) (4)   (3)

Track 58:

(1) 2   3   (+3) (3) 3   (+3) (3) 3   3   (1) 2

Recommended Listening: Jean-Jacques Milteau, Live, Mister Music,1993

Patterns in the style of Sonny Boy Williamson II (1912-1965)

"Something I fell in love with when I was about 12 years old. "The thing was, we were in England and there was a great blues performer called Sonny Boy Williamson …" Mick Jagger

Sonny Boy Williamson II was by far the best blues singer/harmonica player. Though his real name was Willie "Rice" Miller he proclaimed to be the original Sonny Boy. John Lee Williamson (1914-1948), aka Sonny Boy Williamson was referred to by scholars as the first Sonny Boy. He started to perform in 1938 and started to record for Trumpet Records in 1951 with BB King, Elmore James and others. He had a warm and simple approach on the harmonica. We could say less is more while listening to his style.

Track 59:

3   3   3   3   3   3   3   3
6 6 6 6 6 6 6 6 (5) (4) (5) (3) 3   6 6 6 6 6 6 6 6 (5) (4) (5) (3)

Track 60:

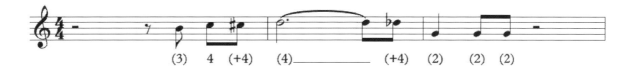

(3)   4   (+4)   (4)_____   (+4) (2)   (2) (2)

Track 61:

(36) (25) (4) (36) (25) (4) (36) (36) (36) (36) (36) (36) (36) (36) (25) 25 (4) 4 (3)

Track 62:

(3) (2) 2 (2) (3) (2) 2 (2)

Track 63:

(5) 5 (4) 4 (4) (5) 5 (4) 4 (4)

Track 64:

(3) (=3) (2) 2 (2) 2 (2) (2) (3) (3) (=3) (2) 2 (2) 2 (2) (2) (1)

Track 65:

3 (3) 4 6 (5) (4) 3 (3) 4 6 (5) (4)

Track 66

(1) 2 3 2 3 (34) (34) (34) (1) 2 3 2 3 (34) (34) (34) (1) 2 3 2

24

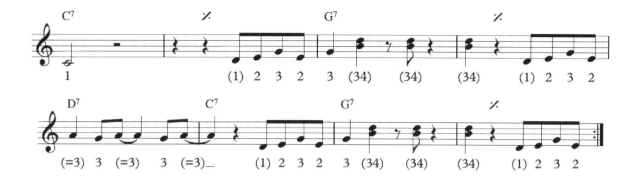

Recommended Listening: Sonny Boy Williamson His Best, Chess, 1997

Patterns in the style of Little Walter (1930-1968)

"Me and my harp was a love affair from way back." Little Walter

Little Walter is widely known to have established the standard vocabulary for the modern blues harmonica. His influence can be heard in virtually every blues harp player who came after him such as Junior Wells, James Cotton, Jean-Jacques Milteau, Carey Bell, Big Walter Horton, Sugar Blue among many others. Little Walter was portrayed in the film Cadillac Records, directed by Daniel Martin.

Track 67:

Track 68:

Track 69:

Track 70:

Track 71:

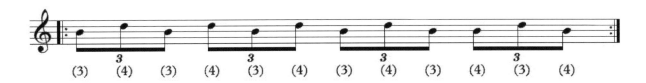

Track 72:

Track 73:

Track 74:

Track 75:

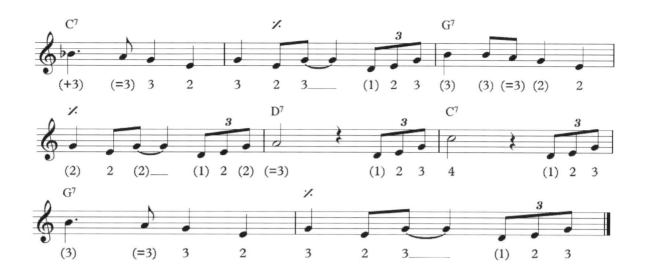

Track 76:

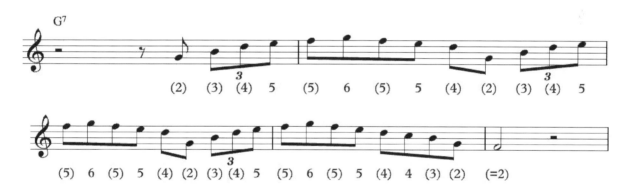

Track 77:

Patterns in the style of Big Walter Horton (1917-1981)

"Sonny Boy Williamson...I taught him half of what he knows." Big Walter

Horton

Big Walter Horton is one of those who laid the foundation of modern blues harmonica of Chicago, he also repeatedly claimed to have been the first to play amplified and early forties. He has played with numerous blues stars such as Johnny Shines, Jimmy Rogers , Otis Rush and Howlin' Wolf and has recorded under his own name for Chess Records and Cobra.

Track 78:

3   3   (3 (+3) (3) (4)   4   4 4 5 6   (7) (7) 6 4 (5) 6____ 6

Track 79:

(4)   6   (4)   4   (3)   (2)   (+3)   (3)_____

Track 80:

3   (+3)   (4)   3   (+3)   (4) (+4) 4 (+3) 3   3

Track 81:

(2) (3) (4)   (2) (3) (4) 5 (3) (2) (+3) (3)   6   6

Track 82:

Track 83:

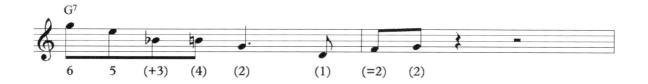

Track 84:

Track 85:

Track 86:

Track 87:

(2)   (2) (+3) (2)   (2) (+3) 4 (+4) 4 (+3) 3   (1) (=2) (1)

Track 88:

(2) (3) (4)____   (3)   4 (4) (+3) (3) (2) (1) (=2) (1)

Track 89:

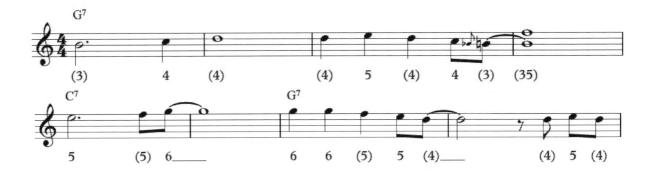

(3)   4   (4)   (4)   5   (4)   4   (3) (35)

5   (5) 6____   6   6   (5)   5   (4)____   (4) 5 (4)

Recommended Listening: Junior Wells, Best of the Vanguard Year, Vanguard, 1998

Patterns in the style of James Cotton (1935)

"The harmonica...It's all about the sound. I liked it. I really liked it...If I don't feel it, I can't play "James Cotton

Besides leading his own band for half a century, James Cotton has played harmonica with Howlin' Wolf and in Muddy Waters' band. He has made more than 100 albums, both as a front man and featured harmonica player. He's been nominated for a Best Traditional Blues Album Grammy six times and took home a statue for *Deep In The Blues* (1996 Verve.) While growing up in Mississippi, he learned the harmonica directly from a certain Sonny Boy Williamson...

Track 90:

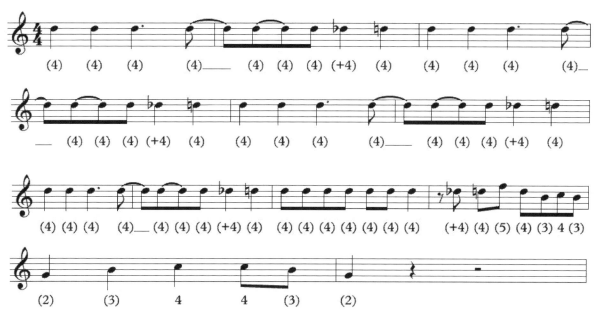

Track 91:

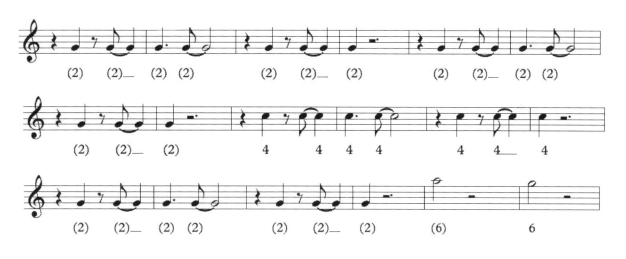

Track 92:

Track 93:

Track 94:

Track 95:

Track 96:

Track 97:

Track 98:

Track 99:

Track 100:

(2)   (+3)   4   (+4)   4   (+3)   (2)

Track 101:

(1) (=2) (1) (=2) (2)   (1) (=2) (1) (=2) (2)   (3)

<u>Recommended Listening</u>: James Cotton, Live From Chicago - Mr. Superharp Himself!, Alligator Records, 2009

Fundamentals Harmonica Scales

There are a few important scales that I recommend to learn in order to improve your technic and wider your musical language   such as The Major, Melodic Minor, Dorian Mode, Mixolydian Mode, Pentatonic, Bebop Major, Bebop Dominant, Bebop Minor, Diminished, Whole Tone and Chromatic Scale. These scales should help you construct your patterns and build your solos. You can see them as a pool of notes to select which will fit with a particular chord or chord progression.

The following scales are written in the key of C. Knowing the scale degrees of each scale will enable you to transpose it more rapidly to another key.

<u>Chords:</u> three or more notes played simultaneously. Usually built from stacked thirds. The 4 chord-tones of a Major 7th are 1 3 5 7.

<u>Scale Degree:</u> Each note in the scale has a specific position and have both a number and a name. Their name relates to their function into the scale. For example in C Major:

Scale Degrees	Name	C Major Scale
1	Tonic	C
2	Supertonic	D
3	Mediant	E
4	Subdominant	F
5	Dominant	G
6	Submediant	A
7	Leading Tone	B

C Major scale/ Ionian Mode

The C Major scale/ Ionian Mode is represented below in two complete octaves. Scale Degrees 1, 2, 3, 4, 5, 6, 7. It works on Major chords and Major chords progressions.

Track 102 | The C Major scale/ Ionian Mode:

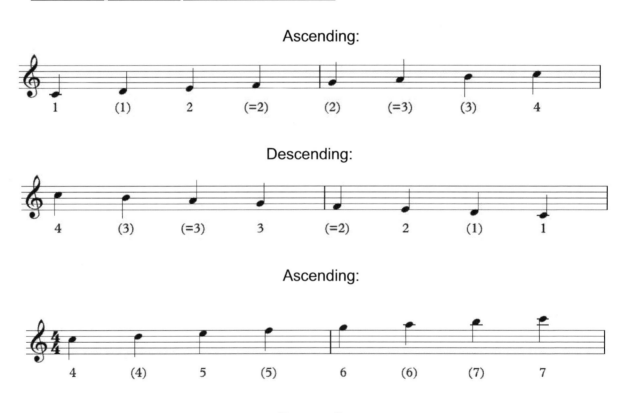

Ascending:

Descending:

Ascending:

Descending:

7   (7)   (6)   6   (5)   5   (4)   4

Track 103 | Preparatory Exercises In the key of C:

It should been practiced in all twelve keys. The goal is to make every key as easy as possible. Take time to work on the difficult ones such as B, E and A major.

C Major scale in third:

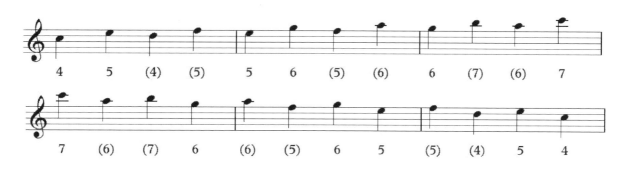

4   5   (4)   (5)   5   6   (5)   (6)   6   (7)   (6)   7

7   (6)   (7)   6   (6)   (5)   6   5   (5)   (4)   5   4

Track 104
Pattern using scale degrees 1, 2, 3 and 5:

4   (4) 5   6   (4) 5   (5) (6)   5   (5) 6   (7) (5) 6   (6) 7   (6) (7) 7   8   (7) 7   (8) (9)

C Major Pentatonic

The C Major Pentatonic Scale is represented below in two complete octaves. Scale Degrees: 1, 2, 3, 5, 6

Track 105 | The C Major Pentatonic Scale:

4   (4)   5   6   (6)   7   (6)   6   5   (4)   4

You can practice the scale starting on the tonic, 3rd degree, 5th degree and 7th

degree. Practice both ascending and descending scale.

G Blues Scale

The G Blues scale is represented below in one octave. Scale Degrees: 1, b3, 4, b5, 5, b7

Track 106 | The G Blues Scale:

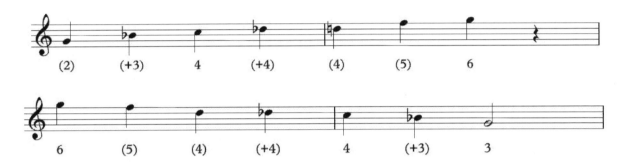

You can practice the scale starting on the tonic, 3rd degree, 5th degree and 7th degree. Practice both ascending and descending scale.

D Minor Melodic scale

The D Minor Melodic scale is represented below in one complete octave. Scale Degrees 1, 2, b3, 4, 5, 6, M7.

Track 107 | The D Minor Melodic scale:

Ascending:

Descending:

(4)   (+4)   (3)   (=3)   3   (=2)   2   (1)

D Dorian

The D Dorian Mode is represented below in two complete octaves. Scale Degrees 1, 2, b3, 4, 5, 6, b7
It is a great mode to use on a D minor blues.

<u>Track 108 | The D Dorian Mode:</u>
Ascending:

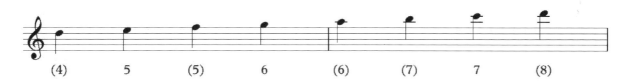

(4)   5   (5)   6   (6)   (7)   7   (8)

Descending:

(8)   7   (7)   (6)   6   (5)   5   (4)

Ascending:

(1)   2   (=2)   (2)   (=3)   (3)   4   (4)

Descending:

(4)   4   (3)   (=3)   (2)   (=2)   2   (1)

<u>Track 109 | Preparatory Exercises:</u>

D Dorian scale in third:

Ascending:

(4)　(5)　5　6　(5)　(6)　6　(7)　(6)　7　(7)　(8)

Descending:

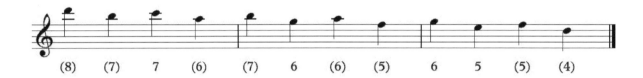

(8)　(7)　7　(6)　(7)　6　(6)　(5)　6　5　(5)　(4)

Track 110
Pattern using scale degrees 1, 2, b3 and 5:

(4) 5 (5) (6) 5 (5) 6 (7)　(5) 6 (6) 7　6 (6) (7) (8)　(7) 7 (8) (9) 7 (8) 8　9

G Mixolydian

The G Mixolydian Mode is represented below in two complete octaves. Scale
Degrees: 1, 2, 3, 4, 5, 6, m7

Track 111 | The G Mixolydian Mode:

Ascending:

(2)　　(=3)　　(3)　　4　　(4)　　5　　(5)　　6

Descending:

38

6   (5)   5   (4)   4   (3)   (=3)   (2)

Track 112 | Preparatory Exercises:
G Mixolydian scale in third:

3   (3)   (=3)   4   (3)   (4)   4   5   (4)   (5)   5   6

Track 113
Pattern using scale degrees 1, 2, 3 and 5:

3 (=3) (3) (4) (=3) (3) 4   5   (3) 4 (4) (5) 4 (4) 5 6   5 (5) 6 (7) (5) 6 (6) 7

C Bebop Dominant

The C Bebop Dominant scale is spelled 1, 2, 3, 4, 5, 6, b7, 7. It derived from the Mixolydian Mode and has a chromatic passing tone between the minor seventh and the tonic. It is represented below in two complete octaves. It is a wonderful scale to use on the C7 chord in a blues in G.

Track 114 The C Bebop Dominant scale :

1   (1)   2   (2)   3   (3) (+3) (3)   4   (3) (+3) (=3) 3 (=2) 2 (1)   1

You can practice the scale starting on the tonic, 3rd degree, 5th degree and minor 7th degree. Practice both ascending and descending scale.

D Minor Pentatonic

The D Minor Pentatonic scale is represented below in two complete octaves. Scale

Degrees: 1, b3, 4, 5, b7

<u>Track 115 | The D Minor Pentatonic Scale:</u>

First octave:

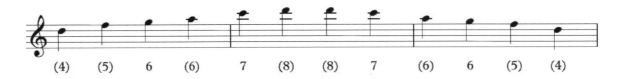

(4) (5) 6 (6) 7 (8) (8) 7 (6) 6 (5) (4)

Second octave:

(1) (=2) 3 (=3) 4 (4) (4) 4 (=3) 3 (=2) (1)

You can practice the scale starting on the tonic, 3rd degree, 5th degree and 7th degree. Practice both ascending and descending scale.

G Major Pentatonic

The G Major Pentatonic scale is represented below in two complete octaves. Scale Degrees: 1, b3, 4, 5, b7

<u>Track 116 | The G Major Pentatonic Scale:</u>

Ascending:

(2) (=3) (3) (4) 5 6

6 (6) (7) (8) 8 9

Descending:

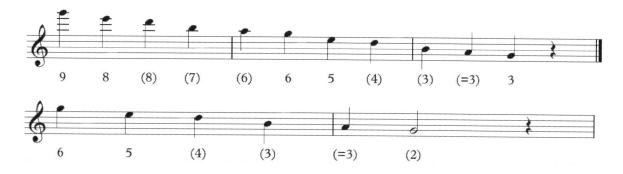

You can practice the scale starting on the tonic, 3rd degree, 5th degree and 7th degree. Practice both ascending and descending scale.

Audio Examples in Mp3 Format Available to Download Here

Enter this link into your browser:

https://nyharmonicaschool.com/audio/

Or

https://goo.gl/MMrP3h

Printed in Great Britain
by Amazon

43236048R00025